LET'S VISIT CHILE

LET'S VISIT CHILE

This is the sixth of John C. Caldwell's *Let's Visit* books about South America and completes his coverage of the half-dozen major nations of that continent. As in all the other books in this best-selling series, photographs are combined with a concise and up-to-date text to give an interesting and accurate portrayal of an important neighbor nation.

Chile is seventh among South American nations in area, fifth in population. Sometimes called the "string-bean country," Chile is 2,620 miles in length from north to south, but averages only 110 miles in width. Within the country are great extremes of climate and geography. The Atacama Desert is one of the world's driest spots, sometimes not having any rain for twenty years. There are other areas with as much as 100 inches of annual rainfall.

The author describes life in country, village and city. He tells of early history and settlement, of Chile's fight for independence, and of naturalist Charles Darwin's Chilean explorations.

In *Let's Visit Chile,* as in all *Let's Visit* titles, Mr. Caldwell discusses the relationship between the country visited and the United States. In this book he particularly emphasizes the fact that the rise of Communist power in Cuba has made understanding and help for our Latin-American neighbors more important than ever before.

Let's Visit Chile

John C. Caldwell

The John Day Company, New York

By John C. Caldwell

    LET'S VISIT ARGENTINA
    LET'S VISIT AMERICANS OVERSEAS
    LET'S VISIT BRAZIL
    LET'S VISIT CEYLON
    LET'S VISIT CHILE
    LET'S VISIT CHINA
    LET'S VISIT COLOMBIA
    LET'S VISIT FORMOSA
    LET'S VISIT INDIA
    LET'S VISIT INDONESIA
    LET'S VISIT JAPAN
    LET'S VISIT KOREA (With Elsie F. Caldwell)
    LET'S VISIT MIDDLE AFRICA
    LET'S VISIT THE MIDDLE EAST
    LET'S VISIT PAKISTAN
    LET'S VISIT PERU
    LET'S VISIT THE PHILIPPINES
    LET'S VISIT SOUTHEAST ASIA
    LET'S VISIT THE SOUTH PACIFIC
    LET'S VISIT VENEZUELA
    LET'S VISIT WEST AFRICA
    LET'S VISIT THE WEST INDIES

By John C. Caldwell and Elsie F. Caldwell

    OUR NEIGHBORS IN AFRICA
    OUR NEIGHBORS IN BRAZIL
    OUR NEIGHBORS IN INDIA
    OUR NEIGHBORS IN JAPAN
    OUR NEIGHBORS IN KOREA
    OUR NEIGHBORS IN PERU
    OUR NEIGHBORS IN THE PHILIPPINES

© 1963 by John C. Caldwell

All rights reserved. This book, or parts thereof, must not be reproduced in any form without permission. Published by The John Day Company, 62 West 45th Street, New York 36, N.Y., and on the same day in Canada by Longmans Canada, Ltd., Toronto.

Library of Congress Catalogue Card Number: 63-10228

MANUFACTURED IN THE UNITED STATES OF AMERICA

0090-0130

Contents

Let's Visit Chile	11
The Land and the Climate	12
Chile's Island Possessions	19
More About the Weather	21
Earthquakes, Volcanoes	23
Before the White Men Came	26
The Wildlife of Chile	28
Discovery and Settlement	32
Chile's Fighting Irishman	40
Chile's Government	48
A Visit to Chile's Cities	52
People of Farms and Villages	57
Travel and Transportation	61
The Spanish Influence	66
The North American Influence	73
Minerals and Industry	74
The United States and Chile	79
The Story of an Earthquake	82
About the Peace Corps	85
Index	95

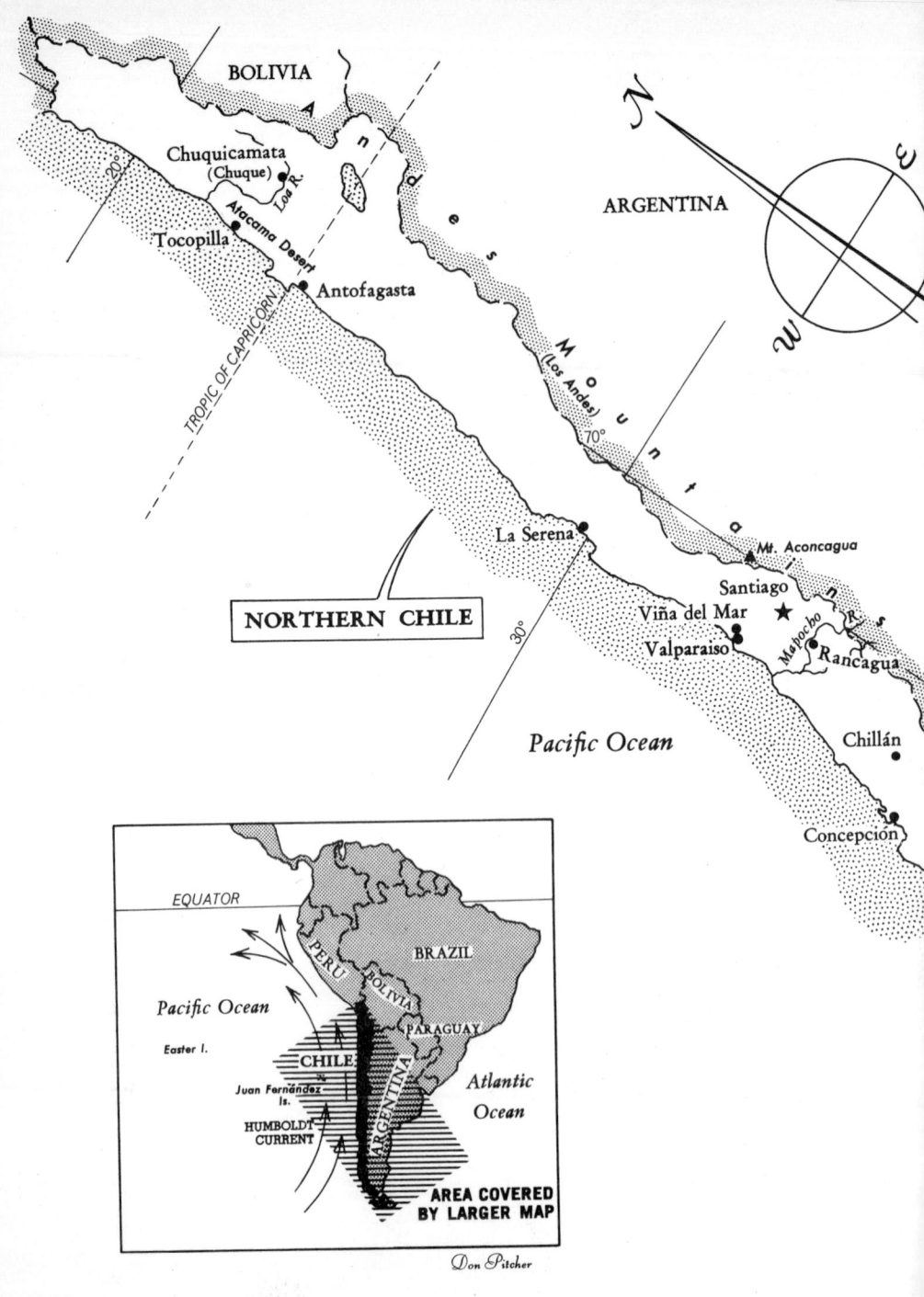

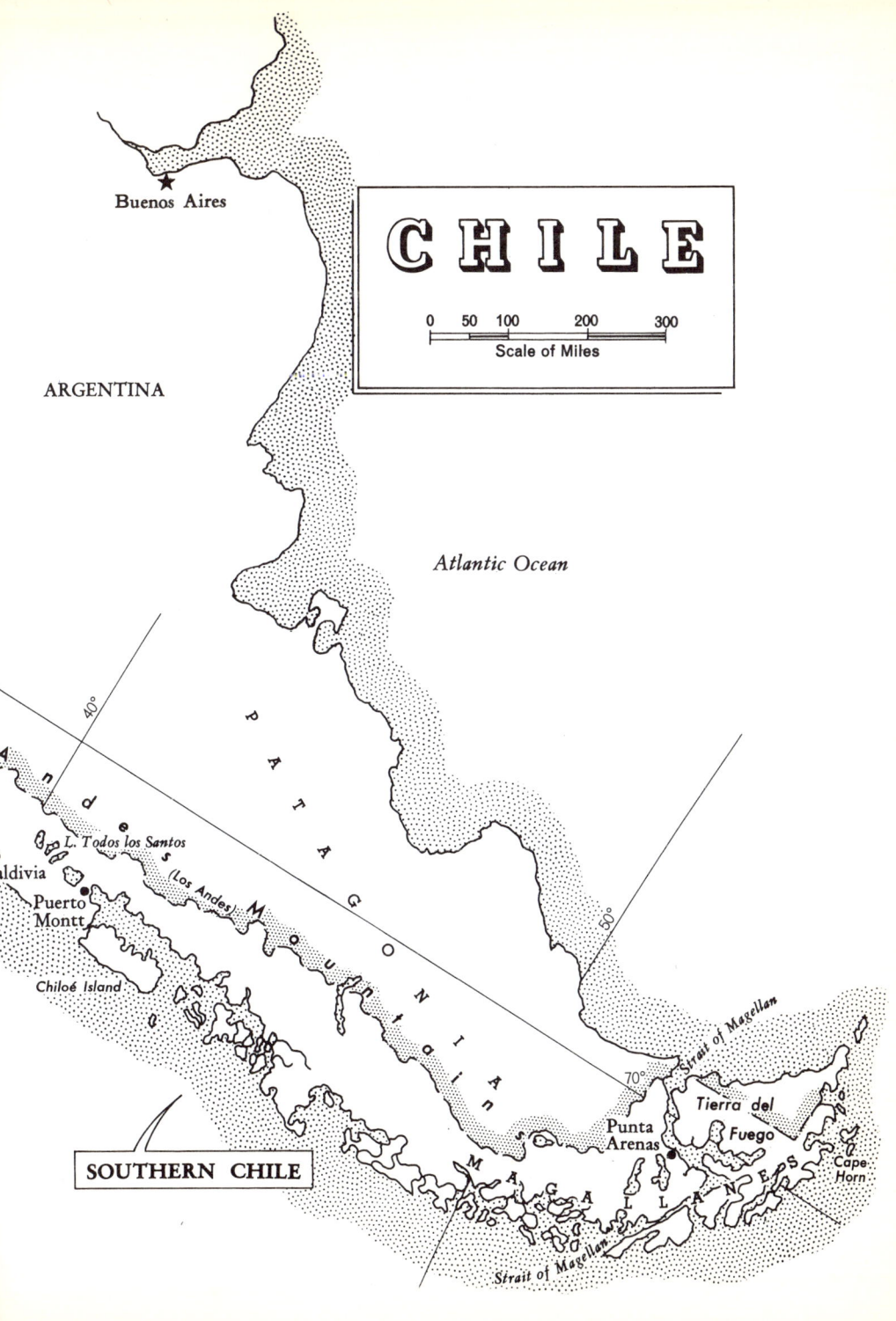

Let's Visit Chile

Chile is sometimes called the shoestring or string-bean country. At no place is it over 250 miles wide, and the average width is only 110 miles. However, from north to south, Chile is 2,620 miles long. This gives the country the longest inhabited north-south length of any country in the world.

The southern tip of Chile is the most southerly point in the Western Hemisphere. The small town of Puerto Williams claims to be the world's southernmost town. Within this long, narrow country there are snow-capped mountains, glaciers, beautiful lakes, virgin forests and one of the world's driest deserts. The highest mountain in the Western Hemisphere is found in Chile. The Atacama Desert, in northern Chile, is surely one of the world's driest places. Sometimes there is not one drop of rain in twenty years!

There are other interesting facts about Chile. It is a land

FLETCHER

The world's driest deserts are found in Chile.

of frequent and sometimes violent earthquakes. During May of 1960, there was a series of earthquakes that took almost 6,000 lives. One of the quakes was so powerful that it created a tidal wave that crossed the Pacific Ocean. When the tidal wave reached Japan, on the other side of the world, it was 35 feet high.

The Land and the Climate

We are not certain how Chile received its name. Perhaps

the name comes from the Aymara Indian word *chilli,* meaning a place where the earth ends. Or the name may come from the Quechua Indian word *tchilli,* meaning snow.

The people who live in Chile do not pronounce the name of their country to sound like something cool, as we do. They say CHEE-leh.

Let's look at the map and locate the string-bean country. We find Chile extends from the southern border of Peru southward beyond the Strait of Magellan. All of Chile's western border is made up of the Pacific Ocean. On the east there is a short border with Bolivia, and the rest of the border runs between Chile and Argentina. This border is almost 2,650 miles in length.

All of Chile is south of the equator. This means that when it is summertime in our country, it is winter in Chile. Seasons south of the equator are the reverse of those north of the equator.

In a country almost as long as the United States is wide, there are of course several differing climates and geographical regions. In the north is the Atacama Desert, where rain rarely falls. It extends from near the Peruvian border for several hundred miles southward. There are numerous rivers flowing from the western slopes of the Andes, but the rivers disappear when they reach the desert. Only one river, the Loa, continues to the Pacific Ocean. The others are swallowed up in the sandy waste of the Atacama Desert.

Were is not for rich mineral deposits, no one would live

in this dry, northern area. However, there are rich deposits of nitrates, copper and borax to be mined. Antofagasta, Chile's fourth largest city, is located in the northern desert, because of the mines there.

South of the desert area there is a middle zone, which consists of a valley over 500 miles in length. We can locate the beginning of this valley by finding Santiago (pronounced Sahn-tee-AH-go) on the map. The valley begins just north of Santiago, the capital city, and extends to Puerto Montt in the south.

The central valley is from 30 to 150 miles wide and has a temperate and pleasant climate. The rich soil is watered

The sea adds beauty to the deserts.

DICK

The Chilean-Argentine lake region is an all-year vacation area.

BRANIFF AIRWAYS

from the rivers and streams flowing from the Andes Mountains. This is a region of fertile farms. And there are also rich mineral deposits in the valley.

The third geographical area begins near the city of Puerto Montt. Inland from this city, the Andes range is cut by rivers and deep valleys. There are large basins created by glaciers many centuries ago. This part of Chile, which extends into Argentina, is often called the Switzerland of South America. The basins made by glaciers are now beautiful lakes. Many of the lakes are connected by clear, fast-flowing streams.

15

DICK

Beautiful Mount Osorno.

It is possible to cross the Andes from Puerto Montt in Chile to Bariloche in Argentina, traveling almost entirely by water. The Chilean and Argentine lake region has become an all-year vacation area. During the winter — which comes in June or July because of being in the Southern Hemisphere — there are skiing and other winter sports. At other seasons there is excellent fishing.* Many years ago the lakes and streams were stocked with rainbow trout from the western United States. The trout have done well in the cold mountain water and now provide wonderful fishing.

On this page there is a picture of Mount Osorno and Lake

* See *Let's Visit Argentina,* by John C. Caldwell (John Day Co., 1962).

Todos los Santos. This mountain is considered the most beautiful in Chile because of its almost perfectly shaped volcanic cone. Many tourists visit this part of Chile to see the reflection of Mount Osorno in Lake Todos los Santos.

As we can see from the pictures, there is heavy snowfall in the Andes. South of Puerto Montt is an area of forests and pastures. The Andes Mountains are lower in the south. Here too there are many lakes. In many ways this part of Chile is like our Pacific Northwest. There are stands of evergreen trees, as in Washington and Oregon.

The area from Puerto Montt south to the Strait of Magellan is called Patagonia. In 1520, when Magellan passed through the strait that now bears his name, he and his men saw the footprints of Indians. The footprints seemed very large, and so they named the southernmost part of the continent Patagonia, or *Land of the Big Feet.*

Across the Strait of Magellan lies Tierra del Fuego, a large island shared by Chile and Argentina. This name means *Land of the Fire Dwellers.* Magellan and his men saw the campfires of Indians on the shore, and so named the island.

The Andes Mountains extend into Tierra del Fuego, but the mountains here are only 6,500 feet high. The climate of Patagonia is cold and wet. Often there is a fifty-mile-an-hour wind that blows day after day. In the southern part of Tierra del Fuego there are many glaciers.

In 1834, the English naturalist Charles Darwin sailed through the Strait of Magellan. Darwin marveled at the harsh climate and wrote that the land was unfit for any but the poor Indians who lived there. However, the southern province of Chile, named Magallanes, which includes Patagonia and Tierra del Fuego, has now become a rich and productive part of the country.

The cold, wet climate has made sheep ranching very profitable. Wool grows thick, and there are sheep everywhere. The provincial capital of Punta Arenas has become the wool capital of the world. In 1945 oil was discovered on Tierra del Fuego. The land which Charles Darwin thought

Wool grows thick in southern Chile.

ICA

unfit for human beings has become an important part of Chile.

While the climate changes from north to south, it also changes from east to west, even though the country is so narrow. Along the whole eastern border is the central chain of the Andes Mountains. The Andes extend north and south from one end of South America to the other.

In the Chilean Andes there are twenty peaks rising to more than 20,000 feet in elevation. Mount Aconcagua, which has an altitude of 22,834 feet, according to Argentina, and 23,081 feet, according to Chile, is the highest point in the Western Hemisphere. This mountain peak is claimed by both Chile and Argentina, because it is located very nearly on the border between the two countries.

To the west of the Andes Mountains there is a long north-south valley. This is the second major geographical region. Then, between the central valley and the Pacific Ocean, there is a range of low coastal hills and mountains.

Chile's Island Possessions

Tierra del Fuego consists of one large and many smaller islands south and east of the Strait of Magellan. Chile also claims other islands. The Juan Fernández (pronounced HWAHN Fer-NAN-dez) Islands lie 400 miles west of the coast of Central Chile. We can locate this island group by finding Santiago on the map. The islands are due west of the capital city. These islands are famous for the fine lobsters caught in nearby waters.

One of the islands is famous for another reason. In the eighteenth century, a Scottish buccaneer named Alexander Selkirk spent eight years on an island named Más a Tierra (Mahs ah Tee-EHR-rah). Selkirk and the captain of his ship had a quarrel, and the Scotsman was put ashore on the lonely island. He was put ashore in 1705, and did not see any other Europeans until 1709. It is said that Selkirk's adventures gave Daniel Defoe the idea for his famous book *Robinson Crusoe*. However, another island also makes this same claim. The people of Tobago,* an island in the Caribbean, claim that Defoe had their island in mind when he wrote the story.

Chile's most interesting island possession lies 2,000 miles out in the Pacific. Called Pascua or Easter Island, this tiny island was once inhabited by Polynesians. The early inhabitants carved huge stone images and scattered them about the island. No one knows at what time the huge images were carved.

The first white men to visit Easter Island killed many of the Polynesian inhabitants. Later, most of the people were wiped out by disease brought by European sailors. The first European explorers were not interested in the stone images and did not try to find out when and why these were built.

---

* See *Let's Visit the West Indies,* by John C. Caldwell (John Day Co., 1961).

Easter Island is visited once in awhile by a mail and supply ship from Chile. Otherwise it is a very lonely place.

The area of Chile is 286,396 square miles, or somewhat larger than Texas. This makes Chile seventh in size among the countries of South America. With almost 7,500,000 people, it is fifth in population.

More About the Weather

We have read about Chile's desert, where rain may not fall for years. And we have also read about the wet and windy islands south of the Strait of Magellan. In a country as long as Chile, there are areas with different climates. Much of Chile's weather is affected by an ocean current that begins in the Antarctic.

Called the Humboldt or Peruvian Current, this great stream of cold water sweeps northward to the coast of Chile and Peru.* This cold current makes the climate of Chile's far north more temperate than we would expect of land just inside the tropical zone. The current also affects the amount of rainfall in northern Chile. Cold air produced by the current blows toward the coast, where it meets warm air that forms over the land. When the cold and warm winds meet, the clouds that are formed are forced upward, and there is no rainfall.

* See *Let's Visit Peru*, by John C. Caldwell (John Day Co., 1962).

The Humboldt or Peruvian Current has even more effect on the climate of coastal Peru. Except for a small area in the north, the whole Peruvian coast is dry and much more temperate than we would expect of land almost on the equator.

The climate of the central valley, south of the Atacama Desert, is temperate. The winters are wet, but temperatures rarely fall below freezing. The summer period, which comes from November through February, is dry but not unpleasantly hot.

Even Patagonia and Tierra del Fuego rarely are *very* cold. This is unusual, when we know that the latitude of Patagonia is about the same as that of northern Minnesota.

Of course it is very cold at high altitudes in the Andes. There are many peaks where the snow never melts.

Rainfall in Chile varies from none at all in the northern desert areas to as much as 100 inches a year in parts of the far south. At Santiago, which is inland, the average yearly rainfall is less than 14 inches. But at the seaport of Concepción, only 200 miles away, there are over 30 inches of rain annually.

In its geography and climate Chile can be compared to the United States. Although our deserts are in the west, and Chile's are in the north, we both have deserts. We also both have snow-capped mountains, areas of evergreen forests, glacial lakes, and a temperate central valley where it is never very cold or very hot.

Chile is unlike other South American countries in that

PAN AMERICAN

Puntiagudo, a volcanic mountain.

it has no jungles. The country is either too far south for jungles or is affected by the cold Humboldt Current.

Earthquakes, Volcanoes

The mountains which extend through Mexico, Central America and the length of South America are "young" mountains. This means that geologically the mountains were formed much later than other mountain ranges. Young mountains are higher than mountains that were formed during earlier geological periods. Young mountains often have active volcanoes, or volcanoes which have been active within the past century.

There are active volcanoes throughout Central America. There are few active volcanoes in the Andes. We can tell from the shape of a mountain when it has been a volcano. On page 16 there is a picture of 8,727-foot-high Mount Osorno. We can tell by its perfect shape that the mountain is an extinct volcano. Mount Osorno last erupted about 100 years ago. Its crater is now filled with ice.

Even though there are few active volcanoes in the Andes Mountains, there is still volcanic action deep in the earth beneath the mountains. During the past 175 years there have been a half-dozen major earthquakes, which result from the volcanic action.

In 1797, an earthquake in Ecuador killed 41,000 people. Peru and Ecuador experienced an even worse earthquake in 1868, in which 70,000 lives were lost. A severe earthquake struck Valparaiso, Chile, in 1906. And during a ten-day period — from May 21 to May 30 — nearly 6,000 people were killed in southern Chile. One quarter of the nation's population was left suffering from cold and hunger.

The trouble started with severe earthquakes; then there were volcanic eruptions. The coast was hit by a tidal wave 24 feet high. In the Chilean lake region whole mountains fell into lakes, and new lakes were formed. Whole villages and fleets of fishing boats were destroyed by the earthquakes, eruptions and tidal waves. The strength of the great eruptions far beneath the surface of the land and ocean was so great that tidal waves traveled across the Pacific all the way to Japan.

I visited the beautiful lake region almost a year after the disaster. Several lakes were still discolored from the volcanic dust that had settled in the water.

Unfortunately, scientists cannot predict when such disasters will occur. It is not possible to give warnings, as in the case of hurricanes. There may not be another series of eruptions and earthquakes for another hundred years. Or disaster might come within a few years.

In another part of this book we will read more about the 1960 earthquake and about how our government helped the people of Chile.

These emergency housing units were built after an earthquake.

ICA

Before the White Men Came

The largest Indian tribe living in Chile before its discovery by Magellan was called the *Araucanian* (Ahr-ow-KAYN-ee-an). It is thought that there were 1,000,000 Araucanians living in what is now Chile and parts of present-day Argentina. These Indians call themselves *Mapuches* (Mah-POO-chays), which means People of the Earth. They were a proud and fierce people who fought the Inca Indian armies that came south from Peru. The Incas were able to conquer the other tribes, but they were never able to defeat the Araucanians.

The Indians also fought stubbornly against the Spanish invaders. It was 250 years before the Araucanians were finally subdued by the Spanish. The last serious Indian uprising came in 1861, at the time of our Civil War. Just as in our West, the Indians were finally defeated and placed on reservations. There are about 130,000 Araucanian Indians who now live in the valleys between Santiago and Puerto Montt.

Indian tribes other than the Araucanian lived in Patagonia and Tierra del Fuego. When Charles Darwin visited the area, he wrote about the Fuegian Indians, saying: "... I do not believe it is possible to describe or paint the difference between savage and civilized man ... it is greater than between wild and domestic animals."*

By this statement Darwin meant that the Indians were

* See *Let's Visit Argentina,* by John C. Caldwell (John Day Co., 1961).

FLETCHER

Indian cave drawings made centuries ago.

uncivilized and primitive. They wore no clothing, or perhaps bits of animal skins. Their homes were drafty wigwams made of broken branches. There were two main tribes in the far south of what is now Chile and Argentina. The *Alacalufe* (Ah-lah-cah-LOO-fay) Indians lived in the islands on the western side of Tierra del Fuego. There were 10,000 members of this tribe, also known as the Canoe People. Now it is thought there may be only about 100 pure Alacalufes left. And only 7 members of the once large Yaghan tribe are known to remain.

The few Indians remaining south of the Strait of Magellan are now cared for by the government or by Catholic missions.

The story of the Fuegian tribes is somewhat like that of some of the tribes in the western United States. The early settlers in Patagonia killed Indians as though they were animals. Land was taken by force; whole villages often were wiped out needlessly. By the time people became humane in their treatment of the Indians, several tribes were almost destroyed.

The Wildlife of Chile

Not having areas of tropical jungle, Chile does not produce as great a variety of birds and animals as is found in some other South American countries. But there are interesting species. We owe much of our knowledge of the animal and bird life found when Europeans first arrived to Charles Darwin, the biologist we have already mentioned.

Darwin was most surprised by a huge bird which he wrote about in these words: "Except when rising from the ground, I do not recall ever having seen one of these birds flap its wings." He was describing the world's largest flying bird, called the South American *condor*. These birds have a wingspread of more than twelve feet! Condors are found throughout the Andes Mountains, but are not as common now as when Darwin wrote about them.

The South American condor.

FLETCHER

The most common large animal then and now is called a *guanaco* (gwan-AH-koe). This animal is related to the camel family. There are four members of this unusual group of animals found in South America and in no other part of the world.

The guanaco is wild and found throughout the Andes. Two smaller members of the family, the alpaca and vicuna (vie-KOON-yah) are famous for their fine, soft fur. The fourth member of the family is called the llama (pronounced YAH-mah, since in Spanish two L's together are given a Y sound).*

Nature has given guanacos an unusual way of protecting themselves. If the animals are attacked, they are able to squirt saliva into the eyes of their attackers. The saliva is

* See *Let's Visit Peru,* by John C. Caldwell (John Day Co., 1962).

29

almost like tear gas. It has a terrible smell and can actually blind an attacking mountain lion.

Llamas do not have this protective device. It is thought that the llama was developed by the Incas of Peru by crossing guanacos with smaller members of that family. Llamas are now a domestic animal like our cattle and horses. They are used to carry loads; their flesh is eaten; their hides are used in making boots and clothing. Llamas are common throughout Peru and Bolivia, but there are a few of the animals in Chile.

In southern Chile, especially south of the Strait of Magellan, there are many ducks, geese and swans. The black-necked swan breeds in the streams and lakes of Tierra del Fuego and Patagonia. After their nesting season is over, the swans migrate north. This is the opposite direction to that in which ducks and geese migrate in North America.

There are lions in the wilder parts of Patagonia and the Andes. These animals are close relatives of the puma or mountain lion found in our western states. Charles Darwin wrote in his journal that he had eaten mountain-lion meat. He described it as tasting like veal.

In 1834, Darwin explored and wrote about a section of Chile near Valdivia. The Valdivian coast is south of Puerto Montt, and because of rainy and misty weather, contains thick forests. Darwin discovered an unusual frog in the forests. The long-nosed frog is strange in appearance and in habits. The male frog cares for the eggs. When the eggs hatch, the tadpoles are kept in the male frog's mouth until they have developed into little frogs.

Darwin also discovered the Chilean *parakeet* in the thick forests of Valdivia. All the other members of the parrot family are tropical. This means that the birds are found only in the jungles in the warm, tropical parts of the world. The Chilean parakeet is not as brightly colored as its jungle cousins.

We have already read that rainbow trout were brought to the Andes from our country. Trout are more easily raised than are most other kinds of game fish. Members of the trout family must have clean, cold water in which to live. The rushing streams and lakes of the Andes provide the right conditions for these fish.

The first fingerlings, or baby trout, were brought to the lakes of Chile and Argentina almost sixty years ago. After a few years the grown trout began to spawn, or lay their eggs. The fish are now more abundant throughout the Andes than in their native home in our western mountains.

The rainbow trout is probably the most traveled fish in the world. It has been taken from the Western Rockies to streams and mountain lakes in New Zealand, Australia, Ceylon, India, Pakistan and Africa. Other members of the trout family, including salmon, have also been stocked in the lakes of Chile. The trout fishing there is so good that many American fishermen visit the Chilean lakes on fishing trips.

Because Chile is in the Southern Hemisphere, the fishing season is different from that in our country. In the United States, trout lay their eggs in November and December. The fish are protected during this time of the year. In the Andes, the spawning season comes during our summertime.

Discovery and Settlement

We have already learned that Ferdinand Magellan discovered Chile, as he sailed through stormy waters, for the King of Spain. Like Christopher Columbus and many other explorers of that time, Magellan was looking for a short route to the spice-producing islands of Asia.

It is interesting to learn how men's desire to have more tasty food has changed history. Throughout the Middle Ages the people of Europe had nothing but salt with which to make their food taste better. Then spices began to come into Europe from Asia.

The first spices — pepper, cinnamon, cloves, nutmeg — were brought from India and the East Indian Islands (now the Republic of Indonesia) overland through the Middle East.

Columbus and many others who followed him believed the land of spices could be reached by sailing west across the Atlantic Ocean. Each of these early explorers discovered some part of the New World. Magellan was the first to find the passage that did lead to the Pacific and to the Spice

Irrigation makes even desertland productive.

Islands. Although he did not live to complete the voyage, his ships were the first to sail completely around the world. During this long journey Magellan discovered Guam and the Philippine Islands. It was in the Philippines that he was killed.

In the 100 years following Christopher Columbus' first trip across the Atlantic, scores of Spanish, Dutch, English and Portuguese explorers set out to find the riches of the Indies. However, most of the explorers did not find any treasures of gold, silver, spices, or precious gems. Except for what the Spanish found in Peru, very little treasure of any kind was discovered. The explorers did find and claim new

33

land for their kings and queens. They also found new homes for thousands of Europeans who for one reason or another wanted to leave their homelands.

As we have read, Magellan and his men first saw Chile when they passed through the stormy straits that now bear Magellan's name. Fifteen years later another Spanish explorer came to Chile.

Diego de Almagro did not come by ship. He and his party traveled overland, down the coast of South America from Peru. De Almagro was a partner of Francisco Pizarro, the conqueror of the Incas in Peru. Although de Almagro was disappointed at the results of his trip to Chile, the King of Spain bestowed the whole "land of Chile" upon him.

The new land was given the name "New Toledo." When, after two years of exploring and fighting Indians, de Almagro found no gold, silver, or any kind of treasure, he and his men started back north to Peru.

Diego de Almagro claimed that the city of Cuzco, the Inca capital where there were treasures, really was a part of the Chile land grant. He and his men claimed Cuzco and started a bitter fight with Pizarro's men. In the fighting, Pizarro's soldiers killed de Almagro. And in return, de Almagro's men attacked Pizarro in his living quarters. Both men died, fighting over the Inca treasures.

This story of Pizarro and de Almagro shows us that the Spanish were greedy and more interested in finding treasures than in anything else. All over South and Central

America and in Mexico, the Spanish looked only for treasures, but only in Peru did they find gold, silver or jewels.

However, although the Spanish *conquistadores* (conquerors) did not know it, in many places they were close to another kind of rich treasure. In the part of South America that is now Venezuela, lie some of the richest oil fields and iron-ore deposits in the world. And under the surface of the land that de Almagro thought was worthless lay rich deposits of nitrates, copper and other minerals.

While Pizarro and de Almagro were fighting over Inca treasures, Pedro de Valdivia left Peru to explore Chile. He had been with Cortez, the Spanish conqueror of Mexico,

Under the desert lie rich deposits of nitrates, copper, oil and iron.

DICK

and then became Pizarro's lieutenant. Valdivia went into Chile with an army of 200 Spanish soldiers and 1,800 Indians.

Pedro de Valdivia had a more difficult time with the Araucanian Indians of Chile than he and Pizarro had in defeating the Inca warriors of Peru.* Unlike the Incas, the Chilean Indians refused to give in. After numerous battles, Valdivia founded Santiago in 1541. Later a second settlement, named La Serena, was established on the north coast of Chile. This settlement could be defended more easily against Indian attack than could Santiago.

It is interesting to know that Santiago was founded in the same year as was St. Augustine, Florida. Our city was also founded by the Spanish, and it is the oldest city in the United States.

In 1647, Valdivia was named Governor of Chile. He continued to establish small settlements. And he had continual battles with the fierce Araucanian Indians. In 1553, the Spanish Army was badly defeated and Valdivia was killed. For a few years Spain's control of Chile was lost.

However, Indians could not hold out long against guns, horses and the other fighting equipment of the white men. Other Spanish soldiers and settlers arrived. The Indians continued to fight until 1640, when there began years of uneasy peace. Chile became a part of the Spanish Viceroyalty of Peru. The Spanish settlers, not finding treasures, began to farm.

* See *Let's Visit Peru*, by John C. Caldwell (John Day Co., 1962).

This is a good place for us to compare Chile's history with our history. It is important to understand that many of our early settlers were well educated. They were often men and women seeking new homes where they could follow their religious beliefs without persecution.

On the other hand, the Spaniards who settled Chile and other parts of Latin America were seeking treasures. Many soldiers without education became settlers. Instead of seeking freedom of religion, the Spanish brought their religion with them and forced it upon the Indians. Indians throughout South America became at least nominal Catholics. Often they mixed their own heathen beliefs with the new religion.

Understanding the difference between the North American and South American pioneers will help us understand why progress in government has been slower in South America than in our country. It will also help us understand how dictators often gain control of countries. Uneducated and illiterate people who cannot read or write are easily misled.

Another interesting difference is that Spanish pioneers frequently married Indian women, while North American pioneers did not. For this reason, many South Americans are known as mestizos, (mays-TEE-zoes) or people of mixed European and Indian blood.

We have read that there are about 130,000 Araucanian Indians in modern Chile. There are over 200,000 people who are more Indian than white in ancestry. There are

FLETCHER

There are large Catholic cathedrals and small Protestant chapels in Chile.

two ways in which Chile's population differs from that of some neighboring countries. First, there are fewer Indians than in neighboring Peru or Ecuador. Also there are no Negroes in Chile. The land was not suitable for plantations, and so very few Negro slaves were brought in by the Spanish settlers. There are fewer mestizos in Chile than in any other South American country, except for Argentina and Uruguay.

The original settlers were all Spanish, and from Spain, Chile has its language, its religion and many customs. Although there is freedom of religion, most of the people are Roman Catholics.

During the nineteenth century, many non-Spanish settlers came to live in Chile. Many Europeans and some Americans, bound for the California gold rush, jumped ships that passed through the Strait of Magellan. Perhaps they were too seasick to continue their long voyages. In this way English, Scottish and French settlers came to southern Chile. During the past fifty years many Yugoslavs also have settled around Punta Arenas.

All through the Chilean lake districts there are people whose forebears came from Germany, Switzerland and Aus-

The Swiss and German settlers built "chalets" in Chile.

BRANIFF

tria. Germans began to come in 1846, invited by the Chilean Government.

In its history and people, Chile is more like Argentina than any other South American nation. Although the majority of people are of Spanish descent, there are many whose ancestors came from England, Ireland, Germany, Italy, Austria and Switzerland.

Chile's Fighting Irishman

At one time Spain's New World possessions extended from our state of California through Mexico, Central America and most of South America, excepting Brazil. The colonies were governed by viceroys appointed by the King of Spain. Spanish rule was often harsh. Except for municipal councils called *cabildos* (kah-BEEL-dohs), the Spanish colonists had no voice in their affairs.

The Catholic Church was powerful. The Church operated what few schools there were in the colonies. There was no freedom of religion. It was almost a necessity for all people to be Catholics.

At about the time of the American Revolution, Spanish colonists began to think and talk about self-government. It was the American Revolution and our Declaration of Independence that had the greatest influence in the desire of the Spanish colonists to become independent.

In 1808, Napoleon Bonaparte invaded Spain and placed

his brother on the Spanish throne. Many of the colonists in the Americas were loyal to the deposed King Ferdinand VII. They began to establish governing groups called *juntas* (pronounced HUN-tah) to represent their king. Such a junta was established in Chile in 1810. The next year the first printing press arrived in Chile, and the first newspaper was printed. This paper began to spread the idea of revolution and self-government.

Among the Chilean patriots there was a Chilean-born Irishman named Bernardo O'Higgins (pronounced O'EE-heens in Chile). O'Higgins' father Ambrosio was among the numerous Irish and English immigrants whose families played important parts in Chilean history. The first O'Higgins was a man of great ability, who became Governor of Chile and Viceroy of Peru. Among prominent Chilean families today there are names like O'Brian, MacKenna, Edwards and Walker.

On July 4, 1811, O'Higgins and a fellow patriot, José Carrera, invoked a congress. A democratic constitution was announced, giving authority to three men. This junta of three men refused to recognize the authority of Napoleon's brother, and remained loyal to Ferdinand VII.

However, O'Higgins was not satisfied with this action. He had studied in England; he had watched events in the United States. O'Higgins demanded that the Chilean colonists should have complete independence from Spain. Carrera joined O'Higgins in taking up arms against the

Spanish royalists, or those people who wanted to remain subjects of the deposed king.

O'Higgins first big battle for freedom was not successful. He and his mob were badly defeated in the Battle of Ranvagua in October 1814. After this defeat O'Higgins and many other young patriots crossed the Andes to join forces with the Argentines who were also fighting for independence.

The Argentinian revolution was started and led by a Spanish officer named José de San Martín (pronounced Ho-SAY day San-mar-TEEN).

San Martín was an unusual man.* He realized that it would do little good for one Spanish colony to become free if Spain were to continue to control other colonies nearby. Beginning his fight against the Spanish in Argentina in 1812, San Martín continued until 1816, when victory was won. On July 9 of that year the people of Argentina proclaimed complete freedom from Spain.

If we are to appreciate San Martín's leadership, we should remember that the border between Chile and Argentina is formed by the Andes Mountains. When San Martín, with O'Higgins' help, decided to fight the Spanish in Chile, they had to lead his army across the Andes. There were no highways at that time. The only crossings were tiny trails and footpaths.

* See *Let's Visit Argentina,* by John C. Caldwell (John Day Co., 1961).

The Spanish generals in Chile thought it was impossible for an army to cross the Andes. If an attack were to come, it must come from the sea, they thought. And the Spanish knew that years would be required to build a fleet of ships able to ferry an army around the tip of South America.

San Martín and O'Higgins believed in doing the impossible, and so they played a clever trick on the Spanish. There were two possible crossing places between Argentina and Chile. San Martín decided to fool the Spanish as to which crossing he and his army might take.

He invited local Indian chiefs to a big party, telling the chiefs that he planned to invade Chile. He promised the

This plaza in Chillán is named after San Martín.

ICA

O'Higgins and San Martín had to cross the snow-covered Andes.

Indians that if they would help him, he would protect their lands and villages. San Martín even told the Indians the exact place he planned to cross the mountains.

Unable to keep this big secret, the Indians began to talk. Some Indians crossed the mountain trails to Chile and told the Spanish about San Martín's plans. The Spanish generals were not worried. Even if the revolutionary army tried to cross the Andes, surely only a handful of men could make it, they thought. Just to play safe, the Spanish did send reinforcements to the area near which the crossing was supposed to take place.

And so in January 1817, San Martín and O'Higgins led their army of revolutionaries across the Andes. First they sent two small forces through the trails and mountain passes which they had told the Indian chiefs would be used. But these men were only decoys. A week later the main army of 5,000 men and 1,600 horses crossed at a different place. Eighteen days were required for the army to cross the mountains, and on February 12, 1817, the Spanish armies were completely surprised and defeated at the Battle of Chacabuco.

Two days later San Martín and O'Higgins led their victorious men into Santiago. San Martín was a better-known man than O'Higgins. The grateful Chileans made him governor of a new free assembly. But the Argentines refused to accept him, and so General Bernardo O'Higgins was proclaimed supreme dictator of Chile. In early 1818, he declared absolute and final independence from Spain.

There were still Spanish soldiers elsewhere in Chile. Another year of fighting was required before the Chilean-Argentine patriots were able to defeat the Spanish throughout southern Chile. There was one serious defeat. But still working together, San Martín and O'Higgins won a final victory on April 5, 1818. O'Higgins was seriously wounded in the last battle.

We might compare San Martín's and O'Higgins' crossing of the Andes with George Washington's crossing of the Delaware River in midwinter. But instead of a few hundred yards of icy water to cross, the patriots of South America had miles of icy mountain trails to cover. In order to travel light, the men took food sufficient for only eight days.

Before we learn more about O'Higgins, let's follow San Martín to his final victory. We have said that he was a man of unusual vision. He realized that Argentina and Chile could not be safe as long as other Spanish colonies existed in South America. The large Spanish army stationed in Peru must also be defeated. And in order to defeat the armies of Spain completely, he must lead another unusual campaign.

Once again José de San Martín and his army of Chileans and Argentines defeated the Spanish by doing what was thought to be impossible. The distance from Santiago, Chile, to Lima, Peru, is about 1,500 miles. It would be a difficult feat to lead an army over this long distance of mountains and desert.

San Martín decided to strike Peru from the sea. The invasion took several years to plan. Many ships were needed to transport an army. And in this campaign San Martín had the help of another unusual South American patriot. Or we should say that an Englishman became a South American patriot leader.

In 1818, an Englishman named Lord Thomas Cochrane accepted the command of the Chilean patriot navy. Lord Cochrane had been an admiral in the British Navy. In 1814,

Admiral Cochrane was accused of the crime of swindling, or obtaining money on false pretenses. The charge against him was untrue, but he was fined a large amount of money, dismissed from the British Navy, and sent to prison for one year. After release from prison, Cochrane joined San Martín in Chile.

In 1820, San Martín's troopships, led by Chilean warships under the command of Admiral Cochrane, sailed from the port of Valparaiso. The fleet that set off to invade Peru consisted of 8 warships and 16 troopships.

The Spanish did not believe it possible for San Martín to gather the ships and men needed for an invasion. Just as they were taken by surprise when he crossed the Andes, they were once again surprised and defeated. Peru was liberated; and, with the aid of Simón Bolívar — a Venezuelan patriot leader — the Spanish armies to the north of Peru were also defeated. All of South America finally was free from Spanish rule.

The life of the British admiral who led the Chilean Navy continued to be interesting. In 1823, Admiral Cochrane joined the patriot navy of Brazil, which was fighting to free itself of Portuguese rule. In 1827, he joined the Greeks who were fighting the Turks. After his many battles, helping people to become free, Cochrane returned to England. The false charges against him were dropped. In 1832, he once again became a British admiral.

The three men who had most to do in leading Chile's fight for freedom were all unusual and led interesting lives. General San Martín, an Argentine, was the military leader. Bernardo O'Higgins, son of an Irish immigrant to Chile, was Chile's own most important military leader. And the third of the three liberators, Lord Cochrane, was for a time disowned and dishonored by his own country.

The story of Chile's revolution is somewhat like that of the North American colonists. In our revolution we also had the help of foreign leaders. A French general named Lafayette and a Polish count named Pulaski did their part in helping in the fight against British rule.

To complete the story of Chile's struggle for freedom, it is of interest to know that a North American also played a small part. The sixteen troopships that sailed northward to invade Peru in 1820 were commanded by an American from New England.

Chile's Government

O'Higgins had been named supreme dictator when Chile declared its independence in 1818. For five years O'Higgins worked to build a secure nation. He created a navy, opened public schools, and encouraged farmers to try new crops and new farming methods. He tried hard to make the remaining Indians of Chile a part of the new nation. Because of O'Higgins' efforts, the Indians of Chile were granted the same rights of citizenship enjoyed by any other Chileans.

In treatment of Indians, Chile was years ahead of the United States. For at the time when the Araucanian Indians were given full citizenship, Indians were still being shot like animals in some parts of our country. Their lands were frequently taken from them; whole tribes were forced to move to new lands.

In 1882, O'Higgins called an assembly to draft a constitution. The public had begun to criticize its dictator hero. There were several uprisings against O'Higgins' government. In 1823, he abdicated, or gave up his office, transferring his powers to the group of men called the junta.

Today old Spanish mansions are used for schools or government buildings.

ICA

Since these first uncertain years Chile has enjoyed long periods of good government. There have been fewer dictators and revolutions than among neighboring South American nations.

Between 1831 and 1871, 4 presidents held office, each for 10 full years. During the next 20 years, 4 other presidents served terms of 5 years each. This is unusual among Latin American countries. Usually there are revolutions, dictators, and periods of bitter fighting between different groups of politicians.

During these years progress was made in many ways. For some time there was a dispute between Chile and Argentina over the boundaries between the countries. In 1902, this argument was settled peacefully. A huge statue, known as the "Christ of the Andes," was erected on the borders. This statue has become a symbol of peace between the two countries which share such a long boundary.

However, there was one period of war with Chile's northern neighbors. This period of fighting was called the War of the Pacific, and lasted from 1879 to 1883. It began because of arguments over ownership of rich nitrate deposits in northern Chile. Bolivia and Chile went to war first; soon Bolivia was joined by Peru. But the two countries were no match for Chile. As a result of victory, Chile secured more territory. The argument over the nitrates that started the War of the Pacific was not settled until 1929. Then, in a final settlement, Chile gave back to Peru some of the territory it had won in 1883.

There have been border troubles between Chile and Bolivia from time to time. In 1962, Bolivia accused Chile of unfriendly acts. This argument occurred because Chile built a dam across a river that flowed into Bolivia. The Bolivian Government claimed that Chile was taking water which rightly belonged to Bolivia.

Also there was a brief period of trouble for Chile after World War I, when there were two *coup d'états* (pronounced koo-day-TAH) in which the president was overthrown. (We use this French term to describe a revolution when several leaders plot and suddenly overthrow an elected government.) In South America, a *coup d'état* is usually headed by army officers.

However, in general our Chilean neighbors have had orderly government. Most of the country's presidents have been able to serve out their terms.

Modern Chile is governed under a constitution that went into effect in 1925. It is much like our constitution.

There are three branches of government — the executive, legislative and judicial. The president is head of the executive branch and is elected by direct vote of the people. He cannot immediately succeed himself.

The congress is made up of a senate whose members are elected for 8 years, and a chamber of deputies whose members serve 4 years. The president's term is 6 years. One unusual fact about Chile's government is that there is no vice-president.

Chile is divided into provinces which are like our states.

Each province is administered by an *intendant* who is appointed by the president for a three-year term. Provinces are divided into departments administered by governors also appointed by the president.

We can see that in local government Chile is different from our country. The people do not elect their own state governors.

The constitution of Chile provides freedom of speech, assembly and religion. Since 1949, women have had the right to vote. Neither soldiers nor priests can vote. Citizens are guaranteed complete freedom of religion. But non-Catholics sometimes have a difficult time. We remember that the Spanish pioneers brought the Catholic religion with them, and that the great majority of people are members of the Catholic Church. There have been times and places where the Catholic majority did not allow members of other Christian faiths to worship freely.

A Visit to Chile's Cities

The capital city of Santiago is often referred to as Santiago de Chile. This is because there is also a city by that name in Cuba. With a population of 1,500,000, Santiago de Chile is South America's fourth largest city. As we know, it was founded in 1541.

Santiago is located on the Mapocho River, inland from the port city of Valparaiso. We can see that the city has a beautiful location. The snow-covered Andes can be seen to the east. There are several popular ski resorts within a short drive of the capital.

Santiago, like other South American cities, has several areas called *plazas*. Every South American town or city has one or more of these parklike areas. There is always a big Catholic church on a plaza and usually a statue of a national hero.

There is a picture of Bernardo O'Higgins Avenue on the next page. Also known as the *Alameda,* this is one of Santiago's principal streets. The picture shows us that there are many modern buildings in Santiago.

There are old cathedrals, theatres, and Spanish-style mansions built long ago. We can see from the pictures that streets are wide and filled with modern automobiles.

The picture of the *Vega Chica,* a downtown market place, shows us too that there are sidewalk stores. Farmers often bring their produce into the market and set up their little stores on the sidewalks.

Valparaiso is Chile's second largest city and most important seaport. Founded in 1536, the city has a population of 225,000. Ships from all over the world visit the busy harbor. The city is built in big steps on the rocky hills that rise from the bay. Different levels of the city are connected by flights of steps and in a few places by elevators.

The business center of the city was almost completely destroyed in the earthquake of 1906. It has been rebuilt on flat land.

O'Higgins Avenue, also known as the Alameda.

Chile's winter playground is located in the mountains not far from Santiago. Near Valparaiso is Viña del Mar, the summer playground. There are wonderful beaches, resort hotels and a gambling casino that attracts visitors from all over the world.

Chile's third and fourth largest cities are Concepción and Antofagasta. Concepción is located in south-central Chile and was the colonial capital in the sixteenth century. It was completely destroyed in one earthquake and partially destroyed in another.

Antofagasta is located in the northern part of Chile. It has a population of about 70,000 and is important as the seaport for the nitrate deposits and the copper mines of the north. Big ships visit Antofagasta, to load the ore and the nitrates. It is such an important business center that planes from the United States make a stop at its big airport.

Antofagasta is in the dry, desert part of Chile. Rain comes so rarely that people have a lot of trouble when it does rain. Because there may not be a drop of rain for several years, roofs are often not repaired. They are full of holes, and a rainstorm gets everything wet.

Other small but important cities are Puerto Montt and Punta Arenas. Puerto Montt is at the southern end of the

The vega chica or market place in downtown Santiago.

ICA

GRACE LINES

Steel production in Concepción, Chile's third largest city.

railroad that runs from north to south through much of Chile. American tourists often visit this little city on their way across the Andes by car and launch. The Andean lake region lies a few miles to the east. Puerto Montt is a seaport through which timber and wool are shipped. We might call it the Little Germany of Chile. The area was settled by Germans many years ago. The older people there still speak German.

Finally we come to Punta Arenas, second southernmost city in the world. Situated on the Strait of Magellan, the city was founded as a penal colony. This means that criminals from other parts of Chile were sent there. Punta Arenas is the capital of Magallanes Province and is the center of Chile's sheep-ranching area. The largest sheep ranch in the world, covering 200,000 acres, is located in Magallanes, which includes Patagonia and the island of Tierra del Fuego.

Because of its geography, Chile's population is concentrated in the valleys of the central section. Over 90 percent of the people, whether in cities or in the country, live in this area between Santiago and Puerto Montt. Only 6.5 percent of the nation's people live in the dry northern provinces. And only 1 percent of the people live south of Puerto Montt.

People of Farms and Villages

If you lived in Chile, you would probably live in a village or perhaps on a farm. Santiago, Valparaiso, Concepción and Antofagasta are the only large cities. There are many small towns, villages and farms.

We have read about Chile's deserts and mountains. There are about 180,000,000 acres of land outside the cities and towns. Of these, over 100,000,000 acres are unsuitable for farming. This is the land that is either desert or very mountainous. Another 30,000,000 acres are in forests. As you can see, this does not leave very much good farmland — only about 50,000,000 acres.

On this page there is a picture which shows how Chileans are trying to develop more farmland. Irrigation is very important. The man in the foreground of the picture is turning a valve so that water will flow into the field.

Since Chile is in the Temperate Zone, farmers grow many of the same crops American farmers grow. Wheat is one of the most important crops. Rice, barley and oats are other important grains. Most farms have fields of beans, potatoes and corn. There are fruit orchards, too, including plums, apples, peaches.

Grapes are among Chile's most important farm products.

Irrigation makes it possible to grow trees in north Chile.

ICA

Each year about 85,000,000 gallons of wine are made from Chilean grapes. The wine is of fine quality and has become famous in South America.

In another section we read about the largest sheep ranch in the world. It is found in Tierra del Fuego. Sheep and cattle are among Chile's most important products. There are many large ranches in the southern part of the country.

Next to its minerals, wool is Chile's most important export. The first sheep were brought from the Falkland Islands, in the South Atlantic Ocean, over 100 years ago. The climate of Patagonia and Tierra del Fuego helps make fine wool. It is cold enough so that the wool grows very thick.

Ranchers and farmers in Chile are learning to use modern methods. On page 89 you can see a picture of many cattle. The cowboys or *huasos* (HWAH-sohs) are vaccinating the cattle against hoof-and-mouth disease. This disease can sometimes strike and kill all the cattle on a ranch.

In the United States, thousands of children living on farms belong to 4-H clubs. In Chile, there are similar clubs. But in the Spanish-speaking countries there are called *Clubes 4C*. The 4C stands for: *cabeza* (head), *corazón* (heart), *capacidad* (capacity or ability), *cooperación* (cooperation). Club members learn to raise better crops, better chickens, pigs and calves. There are exhibits and contests among club members, with prizes for the winners.

When a farm family has enough vegetables or other crops ready to sell, the whole family goes into the nearest town.

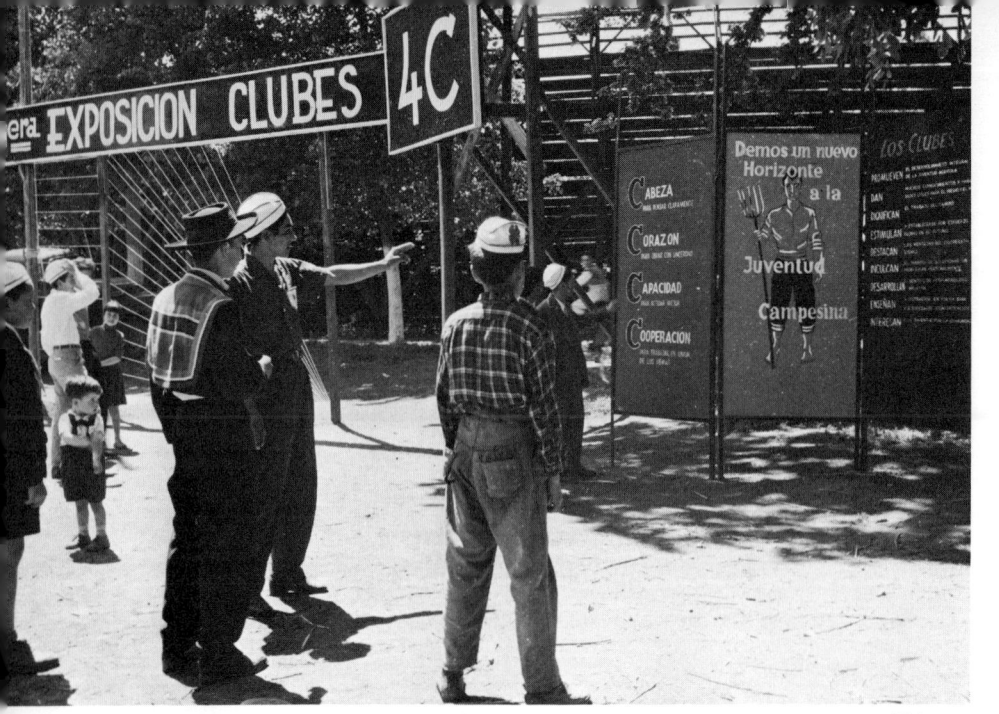

In Chile 4-H Clubs are called Clubes 4C.

There are big outdoor markets where the townspeople can look over the vegetables. While the townspeople are buying their vegetables or meat, the farmers are visiting the stores to buy things they need.

Although there are late-model cars and comfortable buses in Chile's big cities, many farm people still use oxcarts or burros for transportation. In small towns and villages, horse-drawn carriages are still in use.

And although Chile is more modern than several of its neighboring countries, many families in the country areas do not have electricity or running water. If there is a family car, it is very old. With their oxcarts, burros and wagons, farmers can go only short distances.

Travel and Transportation

The first railway in Chile was built in 1849, by William Wheelwright, a pioneer railroad man from New England. It was a short line, connecting a mining town with the ocean. A few years later another American railroad engineer began work on the railroad connecting Valparaiso and Santiago. Henry Meiggs was a New Yorker* and was responsible for many of the railroads that connect the west coast of South America with inland cities. His greatest feat was building the first railroad across the Andes Mountains of Peru.

Building highways and railroads in high mountains is difficult and expensive. Most of Chile's railroad mileage runs from north to south through the central valleys or near the coast. There are several railroads connecting Chile with its neighbors Peru, Bolivia and Argentina. Only one railroad crosses the Andes. Called the Trans-Andean Railway, this line crosses from Los Andes in Chile to Mendoza in Argentina. It is possible to travel from Chilean cities all the way to Buenos Aires, capital of Argentina.

The Pan-American Highway leads from the southern

* See *Let's Visit Peru*, by John C. Caldwell (John Day Co., 1962).

border of the United States, through Central America and the whole length of South America. There are parts of this highway that have not been completed or that are impassable in bad weather. Someday, when all parts of the highway are finished, the long drive will be enjoyed by many Americans. At the present time only adventuresome people with special equipment can make the trip.

When I was visiting the Argentine-Chilean lake region, I met an American family which had made the trip all the way from New York City. They used an amphibious vehicle called a *duck,* developed by our Army.

If there is a family car, it is a very old one.

FLETCHER

ICA

Part of the Pan-American Highway.

In Chile, there are 1,482 miles of the Pan-American Highway, connecting the Peruvian border with Santiago. A branch of the highway crosses the Andes to Mendoza in Argentina. All but about 100 miles of the Pan-American Highway in Chile can be traveled at any time of the year.

In order to develop new farmlands and mineral deposits, Chile must have more highways. New roads are now being built and planned.

We learned that the main railway line ends at Puerto Montt. There are no highways connecting this city with the far southern part of Chile. However, Chile was among the first countries in South America to understand the importance of airlines. There are two Chilean airlines. It is possible to fly to every important city and town, from the border of Peru all the way south to Punta Arenas.

An American airline named Panagra connects Santiago with our country.

The distance from Miami to Santiago is almost 4,000 miles. If you look at a map of the world, you will see that Chile is not only south but also east of most of the United States.

On the opposite page there are two unusual pictures connected with transportation in Chile.

In one picture there is a little railroad handcar. The car has a sail and is pushed along the track by the wind. We might call this a "land sailboat."

The other picture is of a cross along the roadside. In Chile it is the custom to build a cross wherever someone has been killed in a highway accident. Often the crosses are kept decorated by passing truckers and other drivers. Perhaps the placing of these large crosses on the roadside is a good idea. Everyone who passes by sees them, and careless or fast drivers are reminded of what could happen.

The Spanish Influence

We in the United States sometimes forget that the Span-

A train boat.

FLETCHER

A roadside cross.

FLETCHER

iards were in our country long before we arrived to fight the Indians and to form a new nation. The Spanish left behind place names which include three of our states — California, Nevada and Colorado. Among the many Spanish-named cities are Los Angeles, El Paso, Santa Barbara and San Francisco.

There are scores of words in our vocabulary that come from Spanish. Often we sit or play on our *patios*. Or perhaps we might have a *barbecue* in the back yard. Some of us like *chile* sauce. The words *canoe, Negro, tomato* and *potato* and *lasso* are all of Spanish derivation.

Our forefathers who were the earliest explorers in Virginia were surprised to meet Spanish-speaking Indians. It is said that there were fifty bookstores in Spanish Mexico City before our forefathers were civilized enough to have one bookstore. And there were crowded universities in South and Central America 100 years before Harvard Univirsity was even established.

Of course we find Spanish influences and Spanish customs throughout Latin America. Among the independent nations of the continent Spanish is the language of all except Brazil. Among Chileans there are Germans, Swiss, and Yugoslavs who speak their mother tongues in the home; but Spanish is the national language. And of course schoolwork is done in Spanish.

Chile's educational program began during the days of Spanish rule. The Catholic Church established and operated

Schoolgirls wear smocks over their dresses.

all the schools. When independence was won, Bernardo O'Higgins began a program of building at least one school in every town and village.

Of course many years were required before it was possible to have schools everywhere. Since 1920, there has been compulsory education for all children between seven and fifteen years of age. This means that children must go to school. Because of its school regulations, Chile has fewer people who can neither read nor write than does any other South American country.

DICK

Boys wear uniform suits and march in formation.

Since 1928, all elementary-school education has also been free. We have had free education in the United States for many years, but free and compulsory schooling is unusual in many other parts of the world. Because of interest in education, about 80 percent of the population can read and write.

Teaching is in the Spanish language. Boys and girls study the same subjects as are studied by children in our country. Many schools follow another custom that is common in the Spanish-speaking countries. Children wear school uniforms.

As in Spain, the Catholic Church has had a great deal of influence on the lives of the people. The Church operates many schools and colleges. About one quarter of all students attend church or parochial schools. The Catholic church or cathedral is an important part of every city and town. There are many beautiful churches built during colonial times. There are also new and modern churches.

In the United States, most people do not believe that there should be a connection between a religious group and the government. We believe that the church and the state must be separate. Some people believe this so strongly that, in 1962, the United States Supreme Court ruled that school children cannot even be required to say a short prayer.

Chile's constitution also provides that there will be separation of church and government. However, with over 30 percent of the people being Catholics, the Church does have great influence.

In a Catholic country children enjoy many festivals and holidays. Chile's Independence Day, similar to our July 4th, comes on September 18. But there are numerous other holidays and festivals connected with Catholic saints. Often a saint is honored with a *fiesta*. This is a special occasion when people may have processions, feasts and games, as well as special religious services.

Being a Christian people, Chileans celebrate Christmas and Easter. One of Chile's big religious festivals is on January 8. This is the day of the Feast of the Three Kings, when the wise men were supposed to have visited the Christ Child. Especially out in the country, Chileans often celebrate the Feast of the Three Kings. At this time the Christmas tree is taken down, children are given presents, and there is a special mass and a procession.

Another important festival is on September 8. On this day as many as 5,000 pilgrims visit the village of Aiquina in northern Chile, to honor the Virgin Mary. Many Indians walk 100 or even 200 miles to take part in this festival. One year a group of Bolivians traveled on foot seven days to reach Aiquina. Many of the pilgrims wear colorful costumes of red, green, blue and yellow. Hundreds of people dance in the village square, in honor of the Virgin Mary. In the nearby churches thousands of special candles are lit in homage to Mary.

At Easter a figure representing Judas is sometimes hung in the town plaza and burned while the people dance around it. Today this custom is only practiced far out in the country villages.

Chileans follow numerous other Spanish customs. One of these is called the *siesta* (pronounced see-ES-tah). A siesta is a long work break at lunchtime. Instead of going out for a quick lunch, as American businessmen do, Chileans go home for a big, long lunch. Nobody seems to be in a hurry to get back to work. From noon until two or three o'clock, almost everything closes. Many stores, even government offices, close during the siesta.

Since people have a big and sometimes late lunch, dinner also is late. In Santiago and the other big cities, dinner may not begin until nine or ten o'clock. Someone once said that the difference between Americans and Chileans is that the difference between Americans and Chileans is that Americans eat between working hours, while Chileans work between eating hours.

In our country, teen-agers have dates together. They may go to a movie, or to a dance or for a drive in a car. But in Chile, young people rarely go out without a *chaperone*. A chaperone may be an elderly aunt or other relative. The chaperone stays with a couple all the time they are together.

The most popular sports in Chile are those liked in Spain. Soccer, or *futebal* is a game played all over South America. The soccer ball is round, like a basketball. Players score points by kicking the ball through the goal posts. Heads, chest — anything but the hands — may be used in soccer. It is a very fast game and is played by almost all Chilean boys.

Soccer is called *futebal.*

DICK

In southern Chile, rodeos are popular. Chilean cowboys, or huasos, wear colorful clothes for a rodeo. The hat is broadbrimmed and flat. A colorful *manta* also is worn. The manta is just a straight piece of intricately hand-woven material with a head hole in the center of it. It is worn on top of some sort of shirt or jacket, because it does not cover the arms at all. High-heeled boots and fringed leggings that go all the way to the hips complete the huaso's dress.

In a Chilean rodeo the object is to chase a steer around the ring and see how quickly the steer can be forced against a part of the ring that has been padded. This is not like North American rodeos, where the object is either to see how quickly a steer can be lassoed and tied down, or to try to stay on a bucking horse as long as posisble.

There are big rodeos in southern Chile. At Osorno, there is an annual rodeo to select the champion huaso of southern Chile.

Children in Chile play games similar to ours, but with differences that probably come from the Spanish influence or from the Indian. Children play games like marbles and hopscotch and tops. But they whip the tops to make them go around. Boys like to make and fly kites, but they make square kites with one straight stick placed diagonally from corner to corner and a curved stick between the other two corners, allowing the two sides of the kite to give, like "wings," on each side of the straight stick.

The North American Influence

We have learned how Chileans have been influenced by their mother country. The Spanish language, the religion of Spain, many Spanish customs are still followed. Chileans are also beginning to like things North American boys and girls like. Let's see some of these customs that are popular in Chile.

In cities and towns there is always the ice-cream or "good-humor" man who sells ice-cream cones or Eskimo pies. Chilean boys and girls like comic books. They know all about Mickey Mouse and other comic-book and cartoon characters.

Chilean people like American movies. The best-known American motion-picture stars are popular in Chile. Many radio programs that we like in our country are also popular there.

In Santiago there are stores very much like American stores, including supermarkets. In Spanish, a supermarket is called a *supermercado*.

In ways of dressing, our Chilean neighbors are very much like us. The Araucanian Indians and other country people still wear the *poncho* that goes over the neck and covers much of the body. Or some Indians like a large, colorful shawl, but most people dress just as people dress in any North American town or city.

A supermarket is called a *supermercado*.

We find that Chileans and North Americans are really much alike. As modern transportation makes it easier for people to visit one another the differences become less and less.

Minerals and Industry

There is an interesting story about how the Spanish discovered one of Chile's most important resources. Many years ago two countrymen were camped in the northern desert. Soon after they built their campfire the ground around the fire began to burn. The men were frightened by the strange blue flame. The next day they scooped up samples of the earth and took the samples to their village priest. The priest recognized *saltpeter,* one of the ingredients of gunpowder that is found in nitrates. The priest threw the dirt samples into his garden. Within a few weeks the vegetables began to grow faster than any others in the whole area. It is said that this is the way Chileans discovered the life-giving use of nitrates.

The Spanish adventurers who discovered, explored and settled Chile, found no gold or precious stones. For the most part they were disappointed in the waterless Atacama Desert, the dry Andean foothills and the high, cold mountains. But beneath their feet there were real treasures. Chile is more fortunate than its neighbors, because of its great mineral wealth.

Most of this mineral wealth is in the northern part of the country. Chuquincamata, often called *Chuque* (pronounced Choo-kay), is the largest open-pit copper mine in the world. An open-pit mine is one where it is not necessary to dig tunnels and shafts deep into the earth. The mineral is found near the surface.

The open pit at Chuque is 2 miles long, a half mile wide and 1,000 feet deep. This rich mine is located at 9,500 feet, in the Andes foothills. We will find it on the map to the north of Antofagasta.

To the south is El Teniente, the world's largest underground copper mine. The name means The Lieutenant.

This rich copper deposit was supposed to have been discovered by a Spanish Army lieutenant who was a deserter. The nearby town is named Sewell, after Barton Sewell, the American founder of a large copper company.

So far, The Lieutenant has produced ten billion pounds of copper. Chuque has produced another thirteen billion pounds. Chile is second only to the United States in producing this important mineral.

The big copper deposits are found in the mountains or foothills. Beneath the northern deserts lie other riches. The world's only important deposit of nitrates lies beneath the

Copper ingots being loaded.

GRACE CO.

dry and stony wastes of the Atacama Desert. Nitrates provide the life-giving part of commercial fertilizers. Isn't it strange that these life-giving deposits lie beneath the surface of land so dry that nothing can grow on it?

Chile's nitrates are found in the very northern end of the country. Antofagasta and Tocopilla are the seaports from which much of the nitrate is shipped.

If you lived in Antofagasta, you might swim in the sea whenever it was warm enough, but you rarely would take a bath. This is because all the water used by the city has to be piped from the far away Andes Mountains. The precious water is used to keep some grass and trees and flowers growing in the plaza, but hardly anyone can afford the luxury of growing things.

Vegetables are usually shipped from southern Chile and are quite expensive, so people do not eat many vegetables. What a nice place to live — no baths and no vegetables!

In 1850, Chile began to mine enough nitrate for shipment to other countries. The chemical is found in beds about ten feet in depth. Mining is done with big shovels.

In another section we read about the War of the Pacific which was fought between Chile and her northern neighbors in 1879. This war was caused by arguments over who owned the nitrate lands. As we know, Chile won the war and the nitrate.

During World War I, scientists discovered how to make synthetic nitrates. The value of Chile's deposits is not as great now as it once was. However, scientists are busy learning other uses. One by-product of nitrate is iodine. Chile now produces almost 75 percent of the world's supply of iodine.

Chile's copper and nitrate deposits were discovered many years ago. In recent years new mineral wealth has been found. There are rich iron deposits north of Santiago. In the far south there are oil fields in Tierra del Fuego. Chile's oil fields now produce about 9,000 barrels of rich oil each day.

Chile's largest copper mines are owned by American companies. The companies have often been accused of taking the wealth from the ground and not paying enough money. This has caused problems between our countries. Mining in Chile, whether for nitrates in the desert or for copper and iron high in the mountains, is difficult work. During the past few years Communists have sometimes succeeded in persuading the miners that the United States was taking advantage of them. There have been campaigns against the "rich Americans."

However, without American money and knowledge, the rich copper mines might never have been developed. Our country buys almost 80 percent of all the copper produced in Chile. Even this fact sometimes leads to problems. People unfriendly to the United States claim that our big companies do not pay enough money for this copper.

This is a good place to learn more about our relations with Chile.

The United States and Chile

Our Latin American neighbors are less fortunate than the United States. In many countries much of the land is either in jungles, is desert, or is high mountainland. Good crops cannot be grown in areas that are either too hot or too cold. It is difficult to build highways and railways in much of South America. Because of this, there are large areas that have never been properly developed.

We have learned that much of Chile is either desert or lies in the high, cold Andes. Even so, Chile is more fortunate than most of the Latin American countries.

No part of Chile lies in the tropics. This means that some diseases common to the hot parts of the world are not found in Chile. A large proportion of Chile's people can read and write. The country has been fortunate in not having many periods of dictatorship.

Yet there are problems in Chile that need to be solved before its people can enjoy prosperity. The average annual income is very small compared to that in our country. By this we mean the average amount of money made by a man or a family each year.

In the cities there are large slum areas where people live in small, dirty homes without running water or proper sanitation. There are many villages where people do not have running water or electricity. There are large areas of Chile which have not been properly developed yet, because highways have not been built.

The United States has helped the Chilean Government to solve some of these problems. Our government has provided money to build highways and schools. We have sent engineers and other experts to work with the Chilean Government. During the past years we have provided a good deal of economic help.

In spite of its advantages over some of its neighbor countries, Chile has a large number of Communists. Many of the workers in the mines have become Communists. There are also large numbers of Communists in the cities. This is important in the relations between our countries. The Communists teach that the United States is a country which seeks to take over small nations. The economic aid our government gives is often not appreciated. The Communist leaders tell the people that we give help only to get people and countries into our power. The big American companies are denounced by the Communists. Our country and people are often described as *capitalists* whose real interest is in getting control of the resources of other nations.

The problem of Communism is more important now than ever before. During the past few years the government of our neighbor Cuba has become Communist. In 1962, Russia and Communist China began to provide Cuba with arms, airplanes, tanks and many technician soldiers. In late 1962 United States planes spotted rockets in Cuba. These are offensive weapons. The United Nations demanded that the rockets be removed. The Soviet Union replied that she would remove the rockets, but we still wonder if all of them have been taken away.

The Communist leaders of Cuba have bragged that they will help make all the rest of Latin America Communist. We know that the world is divided into two opposing camps. On one side is our country and our free and democratic allies. On the other side are the Communist-bloc nations led by Russia and Communist China. We know that the aim of the Communists is to control the whole world. Communist leaders have said that in time they will "bury" the United States.

The friendship of our Latin American neighbors has always been important, but now, because of the Communist threat, this friendship is more important than ever before. The security of our country would be in danger if all of our neighbors to the south were to come under Communist control.

We have mentioned that economic help has been given Chile. In 1960, a new program to help all our Latin American neighbors was started. Called the *Alliance for Progress,* the aim of this program is to help Latin Americans help themselves. Our government loans money for worthwhile projects. We have agreed to send experts to help Chilean Government experts. Our help includes sending engineers, teachers, farm experts, doctors, and nurses.

In the last two sections of this book we will learn about the special help we have given our neighbors in Chile. One story is about help given in the past; the other is about a program that has only recently started.

The Story of an Earthquake

We have read about the terrible earthquakes and tidal waves that took the lives of thousands of people and destroyed tens of thousands of homes in Chile.

The last great earthquake struck Chile just before dawn on May 21, 1960. First there was a series of giant earthquakes, then tidal waves 24 feet high. These were followed by volcanic eruptions, and within hours, 90,000 square miles of Chile were left in ruins. During the next four days the cities of Concepción, Puerto Montt, Valdivia and Osorno, were left in ruins. Along the seacoast, whole villages disappeared into the ocean.

Within these four days one quarter of Chile's people were either homeless or without food. Railroads and highways were destroyed, so that it was difficult to get help to the destroyed cities and villages. When disaster strikes, destroying towns and villages, there is the problem of providing shelter and food. There is also the danger of disease. It is necessary to give quick help with medicines and trained doctors. Water supplies often become impure. When disease strikes people who are cold and hungry, there may be epidemics that take thousands of lives.

This is the story of what the United States did to help the people of Chile during this time of disaster.

Within a few days a fleet of 74 huge, four-engined cargo planes arrived in Chile, all the way from Fort Bragg in North Carolina, from Fort Belvoir, Washington, and from Dover, Delaware. Within one week our government had flown into Chile:

> 1000 tons of medicine and food
> 800 doctors, nurses and other technicians
> 2 complete 400-bed hospitals
> 12 helicopters, portable radio stations,
> clothing, tents and water purification plants

A field hospital was flown to Chile.

DEPT. OF DEFENSE

DEPT. OF DEFENSE

Army nurses also assisted.

Our President immediately *gave* the people and Government of Chile $20,000,000. Through the American Red Cross and other organizations, another $4,500,000 in help was given.

On July 4, 1960 — six weeks after the terrible earthquake — a special ceremony was held in Valdivia. This city was one of those most heavily damaged. Thousands of people gathered while a Chilean Army band played our national anthem. The mayor of the city had selected four American soldiers to receive special honors and thanks.

The mayor said: "We can never begin to show our appreciation to you and the people of the United States. You have moved into our hearts forever."

The story of American help in time of need is one to be proud of. Perhaps the way our government and people gave help has made friends for us too. Many Latin Americans feel that the United States has slighted them. They feel that we give more help to countries faraway and often forget about our next-door neighbors. We hope that Chileans will remember that time of trouble. We hope the quick way in which our government and people helped will remain in the minds of people when they hear the lies of Communist agents.

Let's hope too that a new program of friendship and assistance will create more friends for us in Chile.

About the Peace Corps

In 1960, a new organization called the Peace Corps began to help Chile and other countries. Many people felt that the Peace Corps would be just one more organization, spending more money to help other countries and perhaps duplicating work already being done. Perhaps this is partly true, but let's end our visit to Chile by reading how this new organization has tried to help our string-bean neighbor.

First let's learn what the Peace Corps is and the idea behind it. This organization is largely made up of young

American men and women who have special skills. There are nurses, farm experts and teachers. Peace Corps workers get very small salaries. They live exactly like the people whom they are helping. By this we mean that Peace Corps workers do not live in American-style homes with American-style food. They do not have servants to help in running their homes.

In Chile the Peace Corps people live in Chilean homes. They study the language and history and customs of Chile before they begin to work. They eat the same food as Chileans eat. And remember that the workers receive very low salaries. In most of the programs to help other countries, big projects are involved. Through our Alliance for Progress Program to help Chile and other Latin American countries, milions of dollars are given or loaned. Our government helps build miles of needed highways or railways; or perhaps a large factory may be built; or a program may include building a big, new hospital.

Members of the Peace Corps help in small but important ways. They live in small towns or villages. Their work is confined to a small area. The job of most Peace Corps workers is to help teach children in school, to bring better farming methods to a small area, or to help solve the health problems in villages or towns. Peace Corps workers are only sent to a country if the government of that country asks for them.

Chile asked for Peace Corps help in bettering the life of its villagers and small-city dwellers. Since 1961, there have

DEPT. OF DEFENSE

Two Peace Corps members look at cabbages they have helped to grow.

been over fifty young Americans helping Chileans solve their problems.

Late in that year, 30 young men and 10 young women were assigned to the project. Their job was to live in rural communities and to help in a community development program. Among the volunteers were young men who had studied animal *husbandry*. This is the science of how to take care of farm animals. Others were specialists in farming. There were several expert carpenters. Among the women Peace Corps volunteers there were teachers and nurses.

87

One of the pictures shows a Peace Corps girl from Indiana teaching a Chilean housewife how to make simple clothes on a sewing machine. Another picture shows a young man and a young women who have been trained in agriculture. It is their job to teach Chilean farmers how to raise bigger and fatter turkeys and chickens, pigs and cattle.

If housewives learn to make clothing at home, their children will be better clothed at less expense. The family will have more money to spend on good food. If farmers learn to feed their chickens better food, the chickens will become fatter and will lay more eggs.

The Peace Corps is interested in better poultry.

DEPT. OF DEFENSE

A U.S. agricultural expert vaccinates cattle.

Peace Corps nurses visit homes and teach mothers how to give their children better care. They give inoculations, teach about first aid and better food.

The kind of help we have described is important in rural areas. In many places there are not enough schools. Most of our Latin American neighbors do not have enough nurses and doctors or agricultural experts. This is especially true in country areas. If people are better fed and in better health, with better clothing, they will be happier and better citizens.

Another Peace Corps project is at work in the poor sec-

DEPT. OF DEFENSE

The Peace Corps helps children.

tions of Santiago and Valparaiso. This is called an *urban community development program*. Another name for this is the YWCA-Chile Project, because Peace Corps volunteers are working with local YWCA's.

In this program young Americans are helping as schoolteachers. The workers live in city areas where people are poor and have poor housing. Some of the workers help combat juvenile delinquency by working with boys and girls from poor families. They forms boys and girls clubs, teach Chilean school children new games and way of having fun.

Many adults in the poor areas of Santiago and Valparaiso are illiterate. This means they never had a chance to go to school and cannot read or write. We know that illiterate men and women have difficulty in getting good jobs. Some of the Peace Corps workers are teaching adult-education classes. Men and women are learning to read and write.

Still other members of this project are teaching uneducated city mothers how to take care of their children. This means teaching about inexpensive diets that are healthful. It also means teaching mothers about health problems and how to make inexpensive clothes at home.

A Peace Corps nurse talks with a patient.

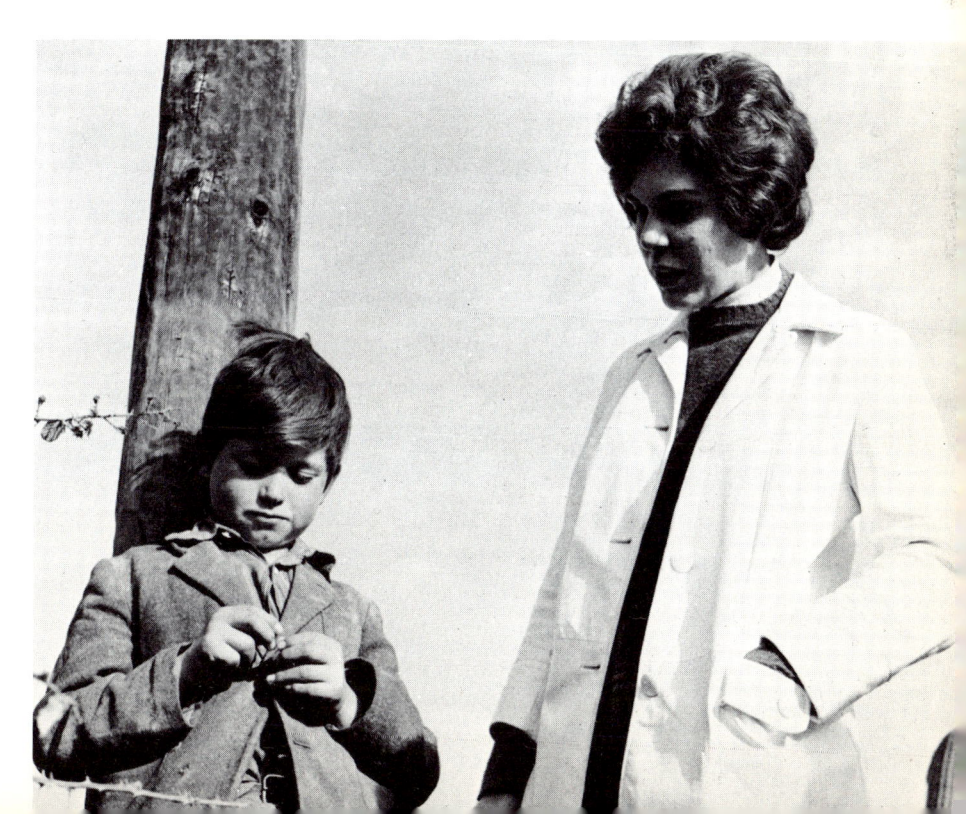

By 1963, there were over 100 young Americans working on Peace Corps' projects in Chile. It is hoped that Peace Corps' projects will be successful, because all the workers are volunteers. We hope that, through the Peace Corps, people will have better health, will be better educated, and will live in better homes. It is also hoped that boys and girls in the cities will have a better chance to become educated and will have better recreational facilities.

And we hope too that through the work of the Peace Corps the many Communists in Chile will have a more difficult time persuading people that Americans are interested only in making money and controlling other countries.

It will be interesting to learn some of the simple accomplishments of Peace Corps workers in Chile and other countries. In Colombia, a young American invented a simple loom for weaving strips of bamboo into latticework over which cement could be placed to make the walls of houses. By building houses this way, the people can keep the cost down and yet have firm walls. The cold air cannot get through the cement-covered bamboo.

In West Pakistan, a young man named Jim McKay taught workers how to lay bricks quickly and properly. It was taking one day for the local workers to lay 125 bricks. McKay taught Pakistanis how to lay that many bricks in five minutes!

During his two years of volunteer Peace Corps work in Chile, a nineteen-year-old boy from St. Louis saw that every child in the mountain section to which he was assigned was vaccinated against polio. He showed the people of several villages how to build a system for pure water. He taught a course in public health to the mothers and fathers of several villages.

Tom Scanlon, another volunteer, worked in a village about forty miles from an Indian village which was proud of the fact that all the villagers were Communists. Several times Scanlon traveled the winding mountain road by jeep, hoping to visit and make friends with the chief.

After Tom Scanlon had made five trips the village chief

A small victim of the earthquake.

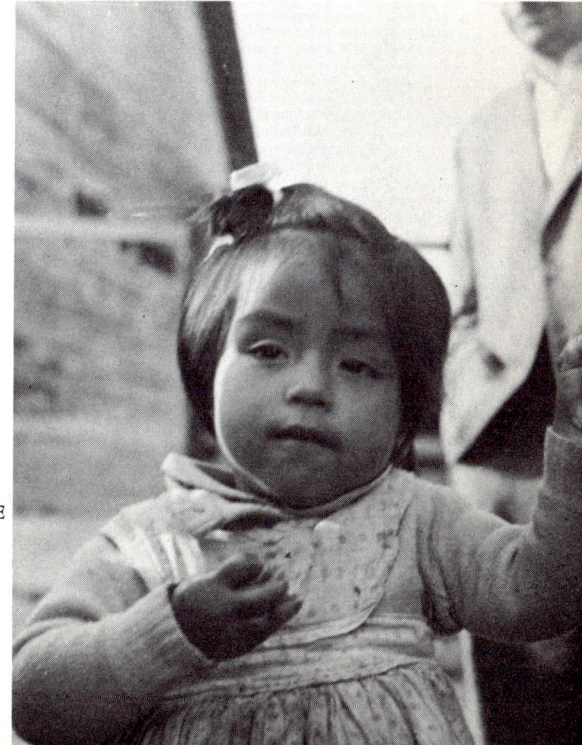

DEPT. OF DEFENSE

finally agreed to talk to the young American. He said: "You are not going to talk us out of being Communists. We know that the Communist way of life is best and that Americans are interested only in making money."

Tom Scanlon replied that he was not interested in talking about Communism, only in finding out if he could help the village people in any way.

The village chief replied: "In a few weeks the snow will come and you will have to park your jeep twenty miles from here and hike through the deep snow on foot. The Communist teachers are willing to do that. Let's see if you are, and then we will talk."

Tom Scanlon waited for the snow. He parked his jeep twenty miles from the village. He hiked through five feet of snow to the chief's house. Then he said: "Let's talk about some of the village problems and see if I can help you." And the chief let him help. Today there are very few Communists in the village, and it is all because of Tom Scanlon's work.

Index

Aconagua, Mt., 19
Alacalufe, 27
Alameda, the, 53
Alliance for Progress, 81
Almagro, Diego de, 34, 35
Andes Mountains, 15-17, 19, 22, 24, 28, 30, 42, 45, 47, 53, 75, 77, 79
Antofagasta, 14, 54
Araucanian Indians, 26, 36, 37, 49, 73
Atacama Desert, 11, 13, 22, 75
Aymara Indians, 13

Bolívar, Simón, 47, 50-51

Canoe People, 27
Carrera, José, 41
Chacabuco, 45
Chile
 area, 21
 climate, 13, 14, 17-19, 21-23
 crops, 58-59
 education, 66-69
 geography, 13-19
 government, 48-52
 name, 12-13
 people, 57-61
 population, 21, 38
 position, 11, 13
 religion, 37, 40, 52, 68-69
 size, 11
 sports, 71-72
 transportation, 61
 wildlife, 28-32
Christ of the Andes, the, 50
Chuquincamata, 75
Clubes 4C, 59
Cochrane, Lord Thomas, 46-48
communism, 80-81, 93, 94
Concepcion, 22, 54, 82
condor, 28
conquistadores, 35
copper, 75-76
Cortez, 36
coup d'état, 51
Cuzco, 34

Darwin, Charles, 18, 26, 28, 30

Defoe, Daniel, 20

earthquakes, 12, 20-21, 23-25, 53, 82-85
Easter Island, 20-21
El Teniente, 75

Ferdinand VII, King, 41
festivals, 69-70
Fuegian Indians, 28

guanaco, 29

Humboldt Current, 21-23

Inca Indians, 26, 30, 34, 36
intendant, 52

Juan Fernandez Islands, 19
juntas, 41

La Serena, 36
Lima, 46
llama, 29-30
Loa River, 13
Los Andes, 61

Magellan, Ferdinand, 17, 26, 32-34
Magallanes Province, 18, 57
Mapocho River, 52
Mapuches, 26
McKay, Jim, 92
Mendoza, 61, 63
mestizos, 37

Napoleon, 40, 41
New Toledo, 34
nitrates, 74-75, 76, 77,
North American influence, 73

O'Higgins, Ambrosio, 41
O'Higgins, Bernardo, 41-49, 67
oil, 78
Osorno, Mt., 16-17, 24, 72, 82

Pan-American Highway, 61-62
Pascua Island, 20-21
Patagonia, 17, 18, 22, 26, 28, 30, 57, 59

Peace Corps, 85-94
Peruvian Current, 21-23
Pizarro, Francisco, 34-36
Polynesian, 20
poncho, 73
Puerto Montt, 14, 15, 16, 17, 26, 30, 55, 56, 57, 63, 82
Puerto Williams, 11
Punta Arenas, 18, 39, 55, 56, 64

Quechua Indians, 13

Ranvagua, Battle of, 42

San Martín, José de, 42-48
Santiago, 14, 19, 22, 26, 36, 45, 46, 52-53, 57, 63, 73, 78, 91
Scanlon, Tom, 93-94
Selkirk, Alexander, 20
Sewell, Barton, 76
Spain, 40, 41, 42, 45
Spanish, the, 26, 41-48
Spanish Influence, the, 64-72
St. Augustine, 36
Strait of Magellan, 17-19, 21, 28, 30, 39

Tierra del Fuego, 17-19, 22, 26, 27, 57, 59, 78
Tobago, 20
Todos los Santos, Lake, 17
Trans-Andean Railway, 61
trout, 16, 31

Valdivia, 30, 31, 35, 36, 82, 83
Valparaiso, 52, 53, 91
Vega Chica, 53
vicuña, 29
Viña del Mar, 54
volcanoes, 23-25

War of the Pacific, the, 50
Wheelwright, William, 61

Yaghan Tribe, 27
young mountains, 23

95

ABOUT THE AUTHOR

John C. Caldwell was born in the Orient and went to school there before coming to the United States to attend college.

Mr. Caldwell went to South China during World War II and spent fifteen months behind the Japanese lines on the China coast. After the war he was transferred to the Department of State and held various positions in a program which has since become known as the United States Information Service.

Since he began writing, Mr. Caldwell has traveled regularly to gather material. He has crossed the Pacific 40 times, the Atlantic 8 times, and has traveled throughout Asia, South America and Africa. He is the author of the *Far East Travel Guide* and the *South Asia Travel Guide* for adults, as well as the *Let's Visit* series and *World Neighbors* series for children.

DATE DUE